Battings

Carry-Along Reference Guide for Quilters and Sewers

Krista Moser

Landauer Publishing

Copyright © 2020 by Krista Moser and Landauer Publishing,
www.landauerpub.com, an imprint of Fox Chapel Publishing Company,
Inc., 903 Square Street, Mount Joy, PA 17552.
978-1-947163-25-6
Printed in Singapore

Contents

History of Batting

Making batting was once very labor intensive. The cotton bolls were picked by hand by family or often slave labor. The cotton bolls had to be dried, with the seeds and debris removed by hand. It was then carded (combed) into small batts. The batts were placed between the layers of the quilt top and back, then very close hand quilting held the layers together.

Wool blankets and extra clothing were often substituted as batting. Eventually the invention of the cotton gin, which separated the cotton from its seeds, made cotton faster and easier to process.

Cotton gin, invented by Eli Whitney (1794)

Know Your Batting

Batting has come a long way from the leftover clothing and blankets women once used. There are so many options. Choose from cotton, cotton blends, polyester, wool, silk, and bamboo. There are various lofts, colors, and sizes to complement your quilt or craft project. Cotton, cotton blends, and polyester are the most popular.

Choose your batting according to the thickness and weight you want. Consider directions for care, cleaning, and shrinkage. Is this batting better for hand or machine quilting? How do you want your stitches to appear and how far apart can the quilting be? How thick or warm do you want the quilt to be? These are all questions easily answered with this handy booklet.

This little pocket guide is intended to give a general overview of the most common batting varieties available and the best uses for those listed. It is always a good idea to read the label on the batting you chose for that brand's specific use and care information.

BATTING TERMINOLOGY

Bearding – Batting fibers separate and may "bleed" or leak through the surface of a quilt between the fabric weave. This can be a problem with darker quilts as a lighter batting will beard through and leave a lint layer across the quilt. It's the most common with wool or silk batting.

Bleaching – Some manufacturers make a bleached version of their battings for use in white or light quilts.

Bonded – Batting treated with resins, glues, or heat fusing the fibers together. This process is often used to retard bearding or prevent fibers from bunching or shifting.

Drape – Pliability of the finished project; soft, flexible, and form fitting.

Fusible – Batting, stabilizer, or interfacing coated on one or both sides with dried glue or resin, which becomes an adhesive when heated.

Loft – Thickness of the batting is called "loft." Generally, the higher the loft the more open the fiber structure. Low-loft batting is thin and flat, high-loft batting is thicker and fluffy.

Needle-punched – The batting fibers are layered up and then thousands of tiny needles are punched through the layers to fuse the fibers together. Sometimes the fibers are needle-punched to a scrim and sometimes they are just needle-punched together with no scrim.

Scrim – A thin layer of woven fibers or mesh applied to the batting to keep the fibers from separating, moving, or lumping together. Often this scrim is made out of polyester.

FREQUENTLY ASKED QUESTIONS

Does Brand Matter?

Generally, batting makers who manufacture similar products are fairly interchangeable. Some, however, set themselves apart by sourcing better-quality goods or by using little or no chemicals in their processing. You can read more about each brand's qualities on their websites.

How is Batting Rated?

Batting doesn't have a rating, per se. Of most common interest is how far apart the quilting can be, how thick the batting is, and how much each batting will shrink.

Which is the Perfect Batting for My Project?

This is dependent on the style of your project and the desired look. Here are some things to consider when looking for the best fit for each project.

- **Use of quilt** – Will this be a bed quilt, wall quilt, table setting, bag, or garment?
- **Laundering** – Will this be laundered frequently?
- **Warm or cool** – Will this be a winter or summer quilt project?
- **Appearance** – Do you want a thin or puffy look?
- **Fiber content** – Do you want natural fiber or synthetic?
- **Quilting** – Will this be hand- or machine-quilted, and how far apart do you plan your quilting stitches to be?

Does Batting Have a Right or Wrong Side?

Officially the answer is no, there is no right or wrong side to batting. That being said, batting does often look different from one side to the other; this is especially the case with needle-punched batting.

The needle-punching process dimples the "top" and punches out the "back." Most quilters want their needle (whether hand or machine quilting) to go in the same direction as the batting was needle punched. This makes the dimpled side the side you put toward the quilt top. The back side (often needle-punched through scrim) is the side that goes against the backing. Having the scrim side against the backing will also help alleviate any bearding, or batting fibers, that might otherwise come through onto the backing.

How Do I Prewash Batting, and Is It Necessary?

Prewashing batting is not typically recommended, but certain battings can be prewashed safely if you want to mitigate as much post-quilting shrinkage as possible. This is especially the case with 100% cotton or cotton blend battings.

To safely prewash/preshrink, soak the batting in a clean bathtub with cool water and little or no detergent. Squeeze out excess moisture by rolling it in a dry towel and then lay it out flat to fully dry. Cotton batting with scrim can be soaked in the washing machine tub without using the agitator, then spun out to remove excess moisture. It can be air-fluffed for 5–10 minutes in the dryer, then laid out flat to dry completely. It is highly discouraged to prewash batting made with silk or wool.

CHOOSING THE BATTING

If the quilt top is 100% cotton, you probably want 100% cotton or another natural fiber batting. Cotton-blend batting, such as an 80/20 mix, is popular for bed quilts. Unless you plan to prewash the batting, you will want to ensure that the fibers shrink at the same rate as the top and backing fabrics.

TYPICAL BATTING MATERIALS

100% Cotton

Made from natural fibers, this type is soft and comfy. It's one of the most commonly chosen batting for all types of quilting and craft projects. 100% cotton batting tends to be very dense and flat.

Cotton Blends

Made from cotton mixed with another fiber, most often polyester. It's typically 80% cotton and 20% polyester. Other fibers such as wool and bamboo are also blended with cotton for a nice effect. Cotton blend batting has the characteristic of cotton batting with a little more loft for a fluffier look. This makes it perfect for bed quilts or anything needing a softer look.

Silk

Typically made with imported silk filaments with the addition of 10% polyester carded or "combed" together and bonded. This makes the perfect light summer-weight quilt while being soft and very easily draped.

BEST-USE CHART

Project Type	100% Cotton	Cotton Blend	Wool
Clothing	X		X
Table Runners, Place Mats, Bags, Totes, Wall Hangings	X		
Throws	X	X	X
Bed Quilts	X	X	X
Art Quilts			X
T-Shirt Quilts		X	
Charity Quilts	X	X	
Baby Quilts, Mats	X	X	

Silk	Bamboo	Polyester	Fusible
X		Low loft	
		Low loft	X
X	X	All lofts	
X	X	All lofts	
X		Low loft	X
	X	Low to medium loft	
		All lofts	
	X	All lofts	

BATTING REFERENCE CHART

Fiber Type	Loft	Shrinkage	Maximum Distance between Stitches
100% Cotton	⅛"–¼" (0.3–0.65cm)	3–5%	4" (10.15cm) (without scrim); 8" (20.3cm) (needle-punched with scrim)
Cotton Blends	⅛"–¼" (0.3–0.65cm)	3–5%	4" (10.15cm)
Silk (90% silk, 10% poly.)	⅛" (0.3cm)	3–5%	4" (10.15cm)
Bamboo	⅛"–¼" (0.3–0.65cm)	Minimal	Up to 8" (20.3cm)
Wool	¼"–½" (0.65–1.3cm)	3–5%	4" (10.15cm)
Polyester	1/16"–⅝" (0.15–1.6cm)	None	4" (10.15cm) avg.
Fusible	⅛" to ¼" (0.3–0.65cm)	Poly, none; cotton/poly 3–5%	4" to 10" (10.15 to 25.4cm)

Hand Quilting	Machine Quilting	Machine Washable after Quilting	Cost
Good	Excellent	Yes, consult label	$$
Excellent	Excellent	Yes, consult label	$$
Excellent	Excellent	Delicate cycle or hand wash; cool temp.	$$$
Excellent	Excellent	Machine wash and dry; cool temp.	$$$
Excellent	Excellent	Delicate cycle or hand wash; cool temp.	$$$
Good	Good	Yes	$
Poor	Good	Yes, consult label	$

Bamboo

Bamboo batting is typically a blend of 50% bamboo and 50% cotton, although there are 100% bamboo varieties available. It is breathable with a slight loft, still warm but lightweight, and ideal for machine quilting. Bamboo is also said to have natural anti-bacterial properties. This makes a great summer-weight quilt or a good bed quilt in warmer climates.

Wool

This type is very lightweight yet warm, and is a natural fiber. Wool batting tends to be higher loft, about ¼"–½" (0.6–1.3cm), making it one of the fluffiest battings in the natural fiber category. Excellent for hand or machine quilting and tying. This batting is perfect for bed quilts or layered with another batting (100% cotton or a cotton/wool blend) to add definition in the quilting texture for show quilts.

Polyester

This is a synthetic fiber that holds its shape and makes some of the highest loft batting available, up to ½"–⅝" (1.3–1.6cm) thick. It comes in a wide range of weights and lofts, from flat and dense to light, airy, and very thick or lofty. It does not compress; it's thicker but lighter. It has warmth without weight, resists mold and mildew, and does not shrink when washed. It is good for bed quilts, comforters, and any project where shrinkage would cause problems.

Fusible

With one or both sides treated with a fusible layer, fusible batting replaces pin or spray basting. The glue is activated by a heated iron so it bonds with your project's fabric. It's best to use this type of batting on smaller projects, such as bags or table runners.

100% Cotton

100% Cotton Batting with Scrim

Clean cotton fiber with a thin mesh (scrim) is needle-punched to the cotton fibers to prevent the fibers from shifting or bunching. This makes 100% cotton batting very stable with minimal stretch and can be quilted further apart than most other battings.

Perfect for bed quilts of all sizes where loft is not desired. It makes great flat and stable batting for wall hangings, table sets, bags, and garments. Many quilters prefer 100% cotton for traditional and heirloom quilting, and it becomes softer with age and washing.

Tends to cling to other natural fibers, making it perfect for domestic machine quilting because it doesn't slide around between the layers while quilting.

Is a very low loft batting, ranging in thickness from $\frac{1}{16}$"–$\frac{1}{4}$" (0.15–0.65cm). Sometimes listed as a weight from 3–6 oz. (85–170g).

Breathable, natural, and sustainable. It retains both cool and warm temperatures.

Does not typically have resins or chemicals to bond it, but the scrim is often made from a synthetic material such as polyester.

Comes in several colors. Choose from natural or bleached white.

Disadvantages
- It does not drape as well as other fibers.
- It is heavier and denser than other fibers.
- Typically shrinks 3–5%, so prewashing is a good idea if you do not want your quilt to shrink much after quilting.
- May be too dense for beginning hand quilters to needle.

100% Cotton Batting without Scrim (Needle Punched)

Clean cotton fiber with no mesh (scrim) is purely cotton fibers layered and needle-punched together. This makes it very soft and pliable. It also makes it more delicate to work with, since it has more stretch and can be easily distorted; even unintentionally, grabbing or gripping the batting may leave dimples where your fingers were. For this reason it should be quilted closer than many other battings (up to 3"–4" [7.6–10.15cm]).

It has many of the same qualities as 100% cotton batting with scrim, with only a few differences.

Softer and easier for hand quilters to needle.

Drapes much better than 100% cotton with scrim.

Shrinks more than 100% cotton with scrim; typically 5–7%.

It is truly 100% natural fiber (organic options available).

Disadvantages
- May stretch or become distorted if handled roughly.
- It is heavier and denser than other fibers.
- Typically shrinks 5–7%; prewashing is not recommended to mitigate shrinkage.
- Can be more expensive than other fibers, depending on the brand and the loft you choose.

100% COTTON BATTING MANUFACTURERS

The batting type sections in this book will contain a list of the popular brands and the products and sizes they sell (craft, crib, throw, etc.) for that batting type. All others that follow for that brand will only list the size type. The products are available at your local craft or fabric retailer and online.

Quilters Dream® Batting

• Natural Dream Cotton Request: Thinnest Loft
PKG. SIZES: Craft 46" x 36" (1.2 x 0.9m), Crib 60" x 46" (1.5 x 1.2m), Throw 60" x 60" (1.5 x 1.5m), Twin 93" x 72" (2.4 x 1.8m), Double 96" x 93" (2.4 x 2.3m), Queen 108" x 93" (2.7 x 2.3m), Super Queen 121" x 93" (3.1 x 2.3m), King 122" x 120" (3.1 x 3m)
ROLL: Runner Roll 18" x 30 yds. (0.5 x 27.4m), Baby Roll 46" x 30 yds. (1.2 x 27.4m), Queen Roll 93" x 30 yds. (2.4 x 27.4m), King Roll 120" x 30 yds. (3 x 27.4m)

• Natural Dream Cotton Select: Mid Loft
PKG. SIZES: Craft 46" x 36" (1.2 x 0.9m), Crib 60" x 46" (1.5 x 1.2m), Throw 60" x 60" (1.5 x 1.5m), Twin 93" x 72" (2.4 x 1.8m), Double 96" x 93" (2.4 x 2.3m), Queen 108" x 93" (2.7 x 2.3m), Super Queen 121" x 93" (3.1 x 2.3m), King 122" x 120" (3.1 x 3m)
ROLL: Runner Roll 18" x 30 yds. (0.5 x 27.4m), Baby Roll 46" x 30 yds. (1.2 x 27.4m), Queen Roll 93" x 30 yds. (2.4 x 27.4m), King Roll 120" x 30 yds. (3 x 27.4m)

• Natural Dream Cotton Deluxe: Weighty Loft
PKG. SIZES: Craft 46" x 36" (1.2 x 0.9m), Crib 60" x 46" (1.5 x 1.2m), Throw 60" x 60" (1.5 x 1.5m), Twin 93" x 72" (2.4 x 1.8m), Double 96" x 93" (2.4 x 2.3m), Queen 108" x 93" (2.7 x 2.3m), Super Queen 121" x 93" (3.1 x 2.3m), King 122" x 120" (3.1 x 3m)

ROLL: Queen Roll 93" x 30 yds. (2.4 x 27.4m), King Roll 120" x 30 yds. (3 x 27.4m)

- **Natural Dream Cotton Supreme: Heaviest Loft**
  PKG. SIZES: Craft 46" x 36" (1.2 x 0.9m), Crib 60" x 46" (1.5 x 1.2m), Throw 60" x 60" (1.5 x 1.5m), Twin 93" x 72" (2.4 x 1.8m), Double 96" x 93" (2.4 x 2.3m), Queen 108" x 93" (2.7 x 2.3m), Super Queen 121" x 93" (3.1 x 2.3m), King 122" x 120" (3.1 x 3m)
  ROLL: Queen Roll 93" x 30 yds. (2.4 x 27.4m), King Roll 120" x 30 yds. (3 x 27.4m)

Hobbs Bonded Fibers
- **Heirloom Premium 100% Natural Cotton with Scrim**
  PKG. SIZES: Craft 36" x 45" (0.9 x 1.1m), Queen 90" x 108" (2.3 x 2.7m), King 120" x 120" (3 x 3m)
  ROLL: 96" x 30 yds. (2.4 x 27.4m), 120" x 30 yds. (3 x 27.4m)

- **Heirloom 100% Bleached Cotton**
  PKG. SIZES: Crib 45" x 60" (1.1 x 1.5m), Queen 90" x 108" (2.3 x 2.7m), King 120" x 120" (3 x 3m)
  ROLL: 96" x 30 yds. (2.4 x 27.4m)

- **Tuscany 100% Unbleached Cotton Batting**
  PKG. SIZES: Throw 60" x 60" (1.5 x 1.5m), Twin 72" x 96" (1.8 x 2.4m), Full 81" x 96" (2.1 x 2.4m), Queen 96" x 108" (2.4 x 2.7m), King 120" x 120" (3 x 3m)
  ROLL: 96" x 30 yds. (2.4 x 27.4m)
  BOARD: 96" x 15 yds. (2.4 x 13.7m)

- **Tuscany 100% Bleached Cotton Batting**
  PKG. SIZES: Throw 60" x 60" (1.5 x 1.5m), Twin 72" x 96" (1.8 x 2.4m), Full 81" x 96" (2.1 x 2.4m), Queen 96" x 108" (2.4 x 2.7m), King 120" x 120" (3 x 3m)

ROLL: 96" x 30 yds. (2.4 x 27.4m)
BOARD: 96" x 15 yds. (2.4 x 13.7m)

- **Tuscany Supreme 100% Unbleached Cotton**
  PKG. SIZES: Throw 60" x 60" (1.5 x 1.5m), Twin 72" x 96"
  (1.8 x 2.4m), Queen 96" x 108" (2.4 x 2.7m), King
  120" x 120" (3 x 3m)
  ROLL: 96" x 30 yds. (2.4 x 27.4m)

Pellon®

- **F – 100% Cotton Batting with Scrim – Needle Punched (93% cotton/
  7% polypropylene scrim)**
  PKG. SIZES: Craft 34" x 45" (0.9 x 1.2m), Crib 45" x 60"
  (1.2 x 1.5m), Twin 72" x 90" (1.8 x 2.3m), Full 81" x 96"
  (2.1 x 2.4m), Queen 90" x 108" (2.3 x 2.7m), King
  120" x 120" (3 x 3m)
  ROLL: 90" x 6 yds. (2.3 x 5.5m), 45" x 75 yds.
  (1.2 x68.6m), 90" x 30 yds. (2.3 x 27.4m), 96" x 30 yds.
  (2.4 x 27.4m), 120" x 30 yds. (3 x 27.4m)
  BOLT: 90" x 9 yds. (2.3 x 8.2m), 96" x 9 yds.
  (2.4 x 8.2m), 120" x 10 yds. (3 x 9.1m)

- **N – 100% All-Natural Cotton Batting, No Scrim (needle punched)**
  PKG. SIZES: Craft: 34" x 45" (0.9 x 1.2m), Crib 45" x 60"
  (1.2 x 1.5m), Throw 60" x 60" (1.5 x 1.5m), Twin
  72" x 96" (1.8 x 2.4m), Full 81" x 96" (2.1 x 2.4m), Queen
  96" x 108" (2.4 x 2.7m), King 120" x 120" (3 x 3m)
  ROLL: 90" x 6 yds. (2.3 x 5.5m), 96" x 30 yds.
  (2.4 x 27.4m), 120" x 30 yds. (3 x 27.4m), 90" x 30 yds.
  (2.3 x 27.4m)
  BOLT: 90" x 9 yds. (2.3 x 8.2m), 96" x 9 yds. (2.4 x 8.2m)

- **G – 100% Bleached Cotton Batting with Scrim – Needle Punched
  (93% bleached cotton/7% polypropylene scrim)**
  PKG. SIZES: Craft: 34" x 45" (0.9 x 1.2m)

ROLL: 90" x 30 yds. (2.3 x 27.4m), 96" x 30 yds. (2.4 x 27.4m)
BOLT: 90" x 9 yds. (2.3 x 8.2m), 96" x 9 yds. (2.4 x 8.2m)

Fairfield™

- **Soft & Toasty™ Natural Cotton Batting (needle punched with scrim)**
  PKG. SIZES: Crib 45" x 60" (1.2 x 1.5m), Twin 72" x 90" (1.8 x 2.4m), Full 81" x 96" (2.1 x 2.4m), Queen 90" x 108" (2.3 x 2.7m), King 110" x 110" (2.8 x 2.8m)
  BOLT: 45" x 5 yds. (1.2 x 4.6m)

- **Toasty Cotton Batting (needle punched with scrim)**
  PKG. SIZES: Crib 45" x 60" (1.2 x 1.5m), Twin 72" x 90" (1.8 x 2.4m)
  ROLL: 90" x 25 yds. (2.3 x 22.9m), 90" x 6 yds. (2.3 x 5.5m), 110" x 25 yds. (2.8 x 22.9m)

- **Purely Cotton™ Batting (100% cotton, needle-punched without scrim)**
  PKG. SIZES: Crib 45" x 60" (1.2 x 1.5m), Twin 72" x 90" (1.8 x 2.3m), Queen 90" x 108" (2.3 x 2.7m)

- **Poly-Fil® Organic Cotton Classic® Batting (bonded, 100% organically grown cotton, needle-punched)**
  PKG. SIZES: Crib 45" x 60" (1.2 x 1.5m), Twin 72" x 90" (1.8 x 2.3m), Full 81" x 96" (2.1 x 2.4m), Queen 90" x 108" (2.3 x 2.7m), King 120" x 120" (3 x 3m)

Bosal™

- **Katahdin™ Premium Quilt Batting (100% natural cotton, Autumn 4 oz.)**
  PKG. SIZES: Crib 45" x 60" (1.2 x 1.5m), Twin 72" x 90" (1.8 x 2.3m), Full 90" x 96" (2.3 x 2.4m), Queen 108" x 90" (2.7 x 2.3m), King 120" x 120" (3 x 3m)
  ROLL: 90" x 30 yds. (2.3 x 27.4m)

- **Katahdin Premium Quilt Batting** (100% natural cotton, Summer 3 oz.)
  PKG. SIZES: Crib 45" x 60" (1.2 x 1.5m), Twin 72" x 90"
  (1.8 x 2.3m), Full 90" x 96" (2.3 x 2.4m), Queen
  108" x 90" (2.7 x 2.3m)
  ROLL: 90" x 30 yds. (2.3 x 27.4m)

The Warm Company®

- **Warm & Natural® Cotton Batting** (100% cotton, needle punched)
  PKG. SIZES: Crib 45" x 60" (1.1 x 1.5m), Twin 72" x 90"
  (1.8 x 2.3m), Full 90" x 96" (2.3 x 2.4m), Queen
  90" x 108" (2.3 x 2.7m), King 120" x 124" (3 x 3.1m)
  BOLT: 45" x 40 yds. (1.1 x 36.6m), 90" x 40 yds.
  (1.8 x 36.6m), 124" x 30 yds. (3.1 x 27.4m)

- **Warm & White® Cotton Batting** (100% cotton, needle punched)
  PKG. SIZES: Crib 45" x 60" (1.1 x 1.5m), Twin 72" x 90"
  (1.8 x 2.3m), Full 90" x 96" (2.3 x 2.4m), Queen
  90" x 108" (2.3 x 2.7m), King 120" x 124" (3 x 3.1m)
  BOLT: 45" x 40 yds. (1.1 x 36.6m), 90" x 40 yds.
  (1.8 x 36.6m), 124" x 30 yds. (3.1 x 27.4m)

- **Warm & Plush™ Cotton Batting** (100% cotton)
  PKG. SIZES: Crib 45" x 60" (1.1 x 1.5m), Queen 90" x 108"
  (2.3 x 2.7m)
  BOLT: 22" x 20 yds. (0.6 x 18.3m)

- **Warm 100® Cotton Batting** (100% cotton, needle punched with scrim)
  PKG. SIZES: Crib 45" x 60" (1.1 x 1.5m), Queen 90" x 108"
  (2.3 x 2.7m)
  BOLT: 110" x 25 yds. (2.8 x 22.9m)

Cotton Blend

Cotton Blend Batting

Cotton blends are made from cotton mixed with another fiber, most often polyester. Other fibers such as wool, silk, and bamboo are also blended with cotton for a nice effect.

Cotton blend batting has the characteristics of cotton batting with a little more loft for a fluffier look. This makes it perfect for bed quilts or anything needing a softer look.

Good for hand or machine quilting, and because of it's open fiber structure, it is especially easy for beginning hand quilters to needle.

It comes in several colors. Choose from bleached white (good for light-colored quilts or quilts with a white background), natural white (good for medium- to dark-colored quilts), and black (good for quilts with a very dark or black background).

Some have as little as 50% cotton, most have at least 80% cotton.

It's perfect for bed quilts of all sizes where a little loft is desired. It has a nice drape and it's durable, stable, and a good choice for quilts that will be gifted where washing and care are not consistent.

Resistant to creases and wrinkles, perfect for quilts that will be folded or stored for a season.

Works well for machine and hand quilting. Close quilting will yield a flat, low-loft appearance, while more space between stitching lines will yield a slightly higher loft. Some brands can be quilted up to 10" (25.4cm) apart (most suggest 4" [10.2cm]).

It is breathable, especially if the blend is with natural fibers (such as wool), and it retains both cool and warm temperatures.

> **Disadvantages**
> - It is not typically 100% natural fiber (unless it is blended with wool).
> - Typically shrinks 3–5%, and prewashing is not recommended to mitigate shrinkage, but there are safe ways to do it if the batting gets soiled.
> - It can beard, depending on the brand.

COTTON BLEND BATTING MANUFACTURERS

Quilters Dream Batting

• Blend for Machines Select Midloft (70% cotton/30% polyester with ultra-light scrim base)

PKG. SIZES: Craft 46" x 36" (1.2 x 0.9m), Crib 46" x 60" (1.1 x 1.5m), Throw 60" x 60" (1.5 x 1.5m), Twin 93" x 72" (2.4 x 1.8m), Double 96" x 93" (2.4 x 2.3m), Queen 108" x 93" (2.7 x 2.3m), Super Queen 93" x 121" (2.3 x 3.1m), King 122" x 120" (3.1 x 3m)

ROLL: Throw Roll 60" x 30 yds. (1.5 x 27.4m), Queen Roll 93" x 30 yds. (2.3 x 27.4m), King Roll 120" x 25 yds. (3 x 22.9m)

BOLT: Baby Bolt 46" x 15 yds. (1.2 x 13.7m), Throw Bolt 61" x 15 yds. (1.5 x 13.7m)

• Natural 80/20 Blend Select Midloft (80% cotton/20% polyester)

PKG. SIZES: Craft 46" x 36" (1.2 x 0.9m), Crib 46" x 60" (1.2 x 1.5m), Throw 60" x 60" (1.5 x 1.5m), Twin 93" x 72" (2.3 x 1.8m), Double 96" x 93" (2.4 x 2.3m), Queen 108" x 93" (2.7 x 2.3m), Super Queen 120" x 93" (3 x 2.3m), King 122" x 120" (3.1 x 3m)

ROLL: Queen Roll 93" x 30 yds. (2.3 x 27.4m), King Roll 120" x 30 yds. (2 x 27.4m)

Three Ways Cotton Blends Are Manufactured

- A thin mesh (scrim) needle-punched to the fibers.
- A slight resin to bond the fiber layers together.
- The fibers are layered up and needle-punched together. These methods all prevent the fibers from shifting or bunching, and make very stable batting that will hold up well through washings. You can get more information on each brand's process on their website.

BOLT: Baby Bolt 46" x 15 yds. (1.2 x 13.7m), Throw Bolt 61" x 15 yds. (1.5 x 13.7m)

• White 80/20 Select Midloft (80% cotton/20% polyester)
PKG. SIZES: Craft 46" x 36" (1.2 x 0.9m), Crib 46" x 60" (1.2 x 1.5m), Throw 60" x 60" (1.5 x 1.5m), Twin 93" x 72" (2.3 x 1.8m), Double 96" x 93" (2.4 x 2.3m), Queen 108" x 93" (2.7 x 2.3m), Super Queen 120" x 93" (3 x 2.3m), King 122" x 120" (3.1 x 3m)
ROLL: Queen Roll 93" x 30 yds. (2.3 x 27.4m), King Roll 120" x 30 yds. (3 x 27.4m)
BOLT: Baby Bolt 46" x 15 yds. (1.2 x 13.7m), Throw Bolt 60" x 15 yds. (1.5 x 13.7m)

Hobbs Bonded Fibers

- **Heirloom Premium 80/20 Bleached Cotton/Poly Blend** (80% cotton/ 20% polyester)
  PKG. SIZES: Queen 90" x 108" (2.3 x 2.7m), King 120" x 120" (3 x 3m)
  ROLL: 108" x 30 yds. (2.7 x 27.4m)

- **Heirloom Premium 80/20 Cotton/Poly Blend** (80% cotton/ 20% polyester; also available in dark blend)
  PKG. SIZES: Crib 45" x 60" (1.1 x 1.5m), Twin 72" x 90" (1.8 x 2.3m), Full 81" x 96" (2.1 x 2.4m), Queen 90" x 108" (2.3 x 2.7m), King 120" x 120" (3 x 3m)
  ROLL: 96" x 30 yds. (2.4 x 27.4m), 96" x 15 yds. (2.4 x 13.7m), 120" x 30 yds. (3 x 27.4m)

- **Tuscany Cotton Wool Blend** (80% cotton/20% wool)
  PKG. SIZES: Throw 60" x 60" (1.5 x 1.5m), Twin 72" x 96" (1.8 x 2.4m), Full 81" x 96" (2.1 x 2.4m), Queen 96" x 108" (2.4 x 2.7m), King 120" x 120" (3 x 3m)
  ROLL: 96" x 30 yds. (2.4 x 27.4m)
  BOARD: 96" x 15 yds. (2.4 x 13.7m)

Pellon

- **Q – 50/50 Wool/Cotton Batting** (needle punched with scrim)
  PKG. SIZES: Craft 34" x 45" (0.9 x 1.1m), Queen 90" x 108" (1.3 x 2.7m)
  ROLL: 90" x 6 yds. (2.3 x 5.5m), 90" x 30 yds. (2.3 x 27.4m)
  BOLT: 90" x 9 yds. (2.3 x 8.2m)

- **D – Dark Blend 70/30 Cotton/Polyester Batting** (needle punched with scrim)
  ROLL: 90" x 9 yds. (2.3 x 8.2m)

- **80/20 Natural Blend with Scrim Batting – Grab N' Go Roll**
  (80% cotton/20% polyester)
  ROLL: 90" x 20 yds. (2.3 x 18.3m)

- **50/50 Light Blend with Scrim Batting (50% cotton/50% polyester)**
  ROLL: 100" (2.5m) width

- **60/40 Natural Blend with Scrim Batting (60% natural cotton/
  40% polyester)**
  PKG. SIZES: Craft 34" x 45" (0.9 x 1.1m), Queen
  90" x 108" (2.3 x 2.7m)

- **E – 80/20 Cotton/Polyester Batting with Scrim – Needle Punched**
  (80% cotton/20% polyester)
  PKG. SIZES: Craft 34" x 45" (0.9 x 1.1m), Crib 45" x 60"
  (1.1 x 1.5m), Twin 72" x 90" (1.8 x 2.3m), Full 81" x 96"
  (2.1 x 2.4m), Queen 90" x 108" (2.3 x 2.7m), King
  120" x 120" (3 x 3m)
  ROLL: 90" x 6 yds. (2.3 x 5.4m), 90" x 30 yds.
  (2.3 x 27.4m), 96" x 30 yds. (2.4 x 27.4m), 120" x 30 yds.
  (3.1 x 27.4m)
  BOLT: 90" x 9 yds. (2.3 x 8.2m) 96" x 9 yds.
  (2.4 x 8.2m), 120" x 10 yds. (3 x 9.1m)

- **A – 80/20 Cotton/Polyester Batting No Scrim – Needle Punched**
  (80% cotton/20% polyester)
  PKG. SIZES: Craft 34" x 45" (0.9 x 1.1m), Crib 45" x 60"
  (1.1 x 1.5m), Throw 60" x 60" (1.5 x 1.5m), Twin
  72" x 90" (1.8 x 2.3m), Full 81" x 96" (2.1 x 2.4m), Queen
  90" x 108" (2.3 x 2.7m), King 120" x 120" (3 x 3m)
  ROLL: 90" x 30 yds. (2.3 x 27.4m), 96" x 30 yds.
  (2.4 x 27.4m), 120" x 30 yds. (3 x 27.4m)
  BOLT: 90" x 6 yds. (2.3 x 5.4m), 90" x 9 yds. (2.3 x 8.2m),
  96" x 9 yds. (2.4 x 8.2m), 120" x 10 yds. (3 x 9.1m)

- **J – 80/20 Bleached Cotton/Polyester Batting with Scrim** (80% bleached cotton/20% polyester, needle punched)
  ROLL: 90" x 30 yds. (2.3 x 27.4m), 96" x 30 yds. (2.4 x 27.4m)
  BOLT: 90" x 9 yds. (2.3 x 8.2m), 96" x 6 yds. (2.4 x 5.4m), 96" x 9 yds. (2.4 x 8.2m)

- **IR – Eco-cotton Reprocessed 70/30 Cotton/Polyester Batting with Scrim – Needle Punched** (70% recycled cotton/30% recycled polyester)
  ROLL: 60" x 60 yds. (1.5 x 54.9m)

- **D – Dark Blend 70/30 Cotton/Polyester Batting with Scrim, Needle Punched** (70% cotton/30% polyester)
  PKG. SIZES: Craft 34" x 45" (0.9 x 1.1m), Queen 96" x 108" (2.4 x 2.7m)
  ROLL: 96" x 6 yds. (2.4 x 5.4m), 96" x 30 yds. (2.4 x 27.4m)
  BOLT: 96" x 9 yds. (2.4 x 8.2m)

- **U – 50/50 Cotton/Polyester Blend Batting With Scrim** (50% cotton/50% polyester, needle punched)
  PKG. SIZES: Crib 45" x 60" (1.1 x 1.5m), Twin 72" x 90" (1.8 x 2.3m), Full 81" x 96" (2.1 x 2.4m), Queen 90" x 108" (2.3 x 2.7m), King 120" x 120" (3 x 3m)

- **K – 60/40 Blend with Scrim Batting** (60% cotton/40% polyester, needle punched)
  PKG. SIZES: Craft 34" x 45" (0.9 x 1.1m), Queen 90" x 108" (2.3 x 2.7m)
  BOLT: 90" x 9 yds. (2.3 x 8.2m)

Fairfield

- **American Spirit Batting™ Superior Blend** (70% cotton/30% polyester, needle punched, light scrim)
  ROLL: 90" x 108" (2.3 x 2.7m)

- **American Spirit Batting Luxury Blend** (50% rayon from bamboo/50% natural cotton, needle punched)
  PKG. SIZES: Crib 45" x 60" (1.1 x 1.5m), Queen 90" x 108" (2.3 x 2.7m)
  BOLT: 90" x 8 yds. (2.3 x 7.3m)

- **Noire® Cotton Blend** (60% cotton/40% special blend polyester)
  PKG. SIZES: Crib 45" x 60" (1.1 x 1.5m), Twin 72" x 96" (1.8 x 2.4m), Queen 108" x 96" (2.7 x 2.4m)
  ROLL: 90"x 20 yds. (2.3 x 18.3m)

- **Machine 60/40® Blend Batting** (60% cotton/40% polyester, needle punched with scrim)
  ROLL: Throw 60" x 60" (1.5 x 1.5m), Super Queen 100" x 116" (2.5 x 2.9m), Super King 124" x 124" (3.1 x 3.1m)

- **Quilters 80/20™ Batting** (80% unbleached cotton/20% polyester batting, needle punched)
  PKG. SIZES: Twin 81" x 96" (2.1 x 2.4m)

- **Noire Cotton Blend** (60% cotton/40% polyester, needle punched)
  PKG. SIZES: Crib, 45" x 60" (1.1 x 1.5m), Twin 72" x 90" (1.8 x 2.3m), Queen 90" x 108" (2.3 x 2.7m)
  ROLL: 90" x 20 yds. (2.3 x 18.3m)

Bosal

- Acadia™ Premium 80% Cotton 20% Polyester Batting (triple carded, needle punched, Autumn 4 oz.)
  PKG. SIZES: Crib 45" x 60" (1.1 x 1.5m), Twin 72" x 90" (1.8 x 2.3m), Full 90" x 96" (2.3 x 2.4m), Queen 108" x 94" (2.7 x 2.4m), King 120" x 120" (3 x 3m)
  ROLL: 120" x 30 yds. (3 x 27.4m), 94" x 30 yds. (2.4 x 27.4m), 120" x 15 yds. (3 x 27.4m)

The Warm Company

- Warm 80/20™ Batting (80% natural cotton/20% polyester, needle punched with scrim)
  PKG SIZES: Crib 45" x 60" (1.1 x 1.5m), Queen 90" x 108" (2.3 x 2.7m)
  BOLT: 110" x 25 yds. (2.8 x 22.9m)

Silk Batting

This type is 90% imported silk filaments with the addition of 10% polyester carded or "combed" together and bonded. It makes the perfect light summer-weight quilt while being soft and very easily draped.

> Super lightweight batting. It is very breathable and is good for garments, lap quilts, or any project where weight would be cumbersome. It is considered low loft batting at only ⅛" (0.3cm).

The fibers are carded (combed) and bonded together to prevent bearding or fiber migration once in the quilt.

Washable once in the quilt or project using cool water on a delicate cycle. It will typically shrink 3–5%.

Is extremely soft and easy to drape and can handle a lot of close quilting without getting stiff. It can also be quilted up to 4" (10.2cm) apart and is good for both hand and machine quilting.

Silk comes from the mulberry silkworm known as *Bombyx mori*. They are cultivated on mulberry leaves, then their cocoons are boiled, the long fibers are extracted, and spun into silk.

Disadvantages
- Typically shrinks 3–5%, and prewashing is not recommended.
- Can be more expensive than other fibers.
- Has a natural, creamy off-white color that may darken quilts with a white background.
- Quilts made with silk batting should be washed in cool water on a delicate cycle.

SILK BATTING MANUFACTURERS

Quilters Dream Batting

• Orient™ Blend Select Batting (mid loft silk, bamboo, cotton, Tencel®)

PKG. SIZES: Craft 46" x 36" (1.2 x 0.9m), Crib 60" x 46" (1.5 x 1.2m), Throw 60" x 60" (1.5 x 1.5m), Twin 93" x 72" (2.4 x 1.8m), Double 96" x 93" (2.4 x 2.3m), Queen 108" x 93" (2.7 x 2.3m), Super Queen 121" x 93" (3.1 x 2.3m), King 122" x 120" (3.1 x 3m)

ROLL: Queen Roll 93" x 30 yds. (2.3 x 27.4m), King Roll 120" x 30 yds. (3 x 27.4m)

BOLT: Baby Bolt 46" x 15 yds. (1.2 x 13.7m), Throw Bolt 60" x 15 yds. (1.5 x 13.7m)

Hobbs Bonded Fibers

• Tuscany Collection Silk Batting (90% silk/10% polyester-resin bonded)

PKG. SIZES: Crib 45" x 60" (1.1 x 1.5m), Throw 60" x 60" (1.5 x 1.5m), Twin 72" x 96" (1.8 x 2.4m), Full 81" x 96" (2.1 x 2.4m), Queen 96" x 108" (2.4 x 2.7m), King 120" x 120" (3 x 3m)

ROLL: 96" x 30 yds. (2.4 x 27.4m)

BOARD: 96" x 10 yds. (2.4 x 9.1m)

Bamboo

Bamboo Batting

Bamboo batting is typically a blend of 50% bamboo and 50% cotton, although there are 100% bamboo varieties available. It is breathable with a slight loft, warm, lightweight, and ideal for machine quilting. Bamboo is also said to have natural anti-bacterial properties. This makes a great summer-weight quilt or a good bed quilt in warmer climates.

Bamboo is a highly sustainable resource and the fastest growing plant on the planet growing 3' (0.9m) in 24 hours. In a perfect climate, it reaches maturity in 3–5 years.

Bamboo batting has natural anti-bacterial properties.

Is considered a low loft batting at only ¹⁄₁₆"–⅛" (0.2–0.3cm) thick. It drapes even better than cotton battings.

Is priced in the midrange, comparable to cotton.

Is breathable, made of natural fiber, soft, and very lightweight. It can be used for any type of quilt garment or project. It is exceptional for machine quilting.

Has minimal shrinkage at 2–3%.

The fibers are typically needle punched through a lightweight scrim for stability. Some processes just needle-punch the fiber together, making these bamboo options a little softer with more drape, although they may also have more stretch than the options with scrim.

Is very stable and can be quilted up to 8"–10" (20.3–25.4cm) apart. It is excellent for machine quilting and can be hand quilted with a little experience.

Disadvantages
- Typically shrinks 2–3%, and prewashing is not recommended.
- Has a natural, creamy off-white color that may darken quilts with a white background.
- Bamboo batting needle-punched with scrim may be harder for newer hand quilters to "needle."

BAMBOO BATTING MANUFACTURERS

Pellon

- **B – 50/50 Bamboo/Cotton Batting with Scrim – Needle Punched** (50% bamboo/50% cotton)
  PKG. SIZES: Craft 34" x 45" (0.9 x 1.1m), Crib 45" x 60" (1.1 x 1.5m), Throw 60" x 60" (1.5 x 1.5m), Twin 72" x 96" (1.8 x 2.4m), Full 81" x 96" (2.1 x 2.4m), Queen 96" x 108" (2.4 x 2.7m)
  ROLL: 90" x 6 yds. (2.3 x 5.5m), 90" x 30 yds. (2.3 x 27.4m), 96" x 30 yds. (2.4 x 27.4m)
  BOLT: 90" x 9 yds. (2.3 x 8.2m), 96" x 9 yds. (2.4 x 8.2m)

Fairfield

- **Nature-Fil™ Bamboo Blend Batting (50% rayon/50% certified organic cotton)**
  PKG. SIZES: Throw 60" x 60" (1.5 x 1.5m), Twin 72" x 90" (1.8 x 2.3m), Full 81" x 96" (2.1 x 2.4cm), Queen 90" x 100" (2.3 x 2.5m)
  ROLL: 90" x 6 yds. (2.3 x 5.5m)
  BOLT: 45" x 10 yds. (1.1 x 9.1m)

- **American Spirit Batting™ Classic Cotton Batting (needle punched, 50% rayon from bamboo)**
  PKG. SIZES: Crib 45" x 60" (1.2 x 1.5m), Queen 90" x 108" (2.4 x 2.7m)
  BOLT: 90" x 8 yds. (2.3 x 7.3m)

- **American Spirit Batting Luxury Blend (50% rayon from bamboo/ 50% natural cotton, needle punched)**
  PKG. SIZES: Crib 45" x 60" (1.1 x 1.5m), Queen 90" x 108" (2.3 x 2.7m)
  BOLT: 90" x 8 yds. (2.3 x 7.3m)

Wool

Wool Batting

Wool batting is very lightweight, yet warm, and is a natural fiber. This batting tends to be higher loft (about ¼"–½" [0.6–1.3cm]) making it one of the fluffiest battings in the natural fiber category.

Wool batting is excellent for hand or machine quilting and tying and is perfect for bed quilts or layered with another batting (100% cotton or a cotton blend) to add definition in the quilting texture for show quilts.

Very popular among hand quilters because the openness of the fibers make it easy to needle. This openness gives it a beautiful drape once in a quilt.

It's crease resistant and has no memory retention when folded or stored, even for long periods of time. This makes it perfect for show quilts that need to look fresh for display or bed quilts that get packed away for a season or two.

The warmest of the batting fibers, it absorbs moisture, is very breathable, and has a wicking effect, moving any moisture out and away from the body. This makes it perfect for cool or damp climates.

Is carded (combed) and bonded to prevent bearding or fiber migration once in the quilt. Some brands use a resin bond while others use a thermal bond process with low-melt polyester. Most brands suggest quilting up to 4" (10.2cm) apart with some allowing for up to 8" (20.3cm) between stitch lines.

Even though it can be more expensive than cotton or polyester batting, you will want a good-quality wool batting and that can be pricey. Look for wool that has been washed well for cleanliness and to prevent as much shrinkage as possible post-quilting. Most wool battings will still shrink 3–5% once washed after they are in a quilt.

Very lightweight, yet lofty. This unique characteristic makes it a great choice for bed quilts if a comforter look is desired. The loftiness also accentuates the quilting texture, this makes it a top choice for show quilts, often layered with a higher density batting such as a wool/cotton blend.

Disadvantages

- Typically shrinks 3–5%, and prewashing is not recommended.

- Can be more expensive than other fibers.

- Has a natural, creamy light yellow color that may darken quilts with a white background.

- Should not be ironed.

- Requires a delicate washing process. Once sewn into a quilt, wash in cool water and air fluff for a few minutes then lay flat to dry.

WOOL BATTING MANUFACTURERS

Quilters Dream Batting

• Dream Wool™ Batting (thermally bonded blend of merino and domestic wool)

PKG. SIZES: Craft 46" x 36" (1.2 x 0.9m), Crib 60"x 46" (1.5 x 1.2m), Throw 60" x 60" (1.5 x 1.5m), Twin 93" x 72" (2.4 x 1.8m), Double 96" x 93" (2.4 x 2.3m), Queen 108" x 93" (2.7 x 2.4m), Super Queen 121" x 93" (3.1 x 2.4m), King 122" x 120" (3.1 x 3m)

ROLL: Queen 93" x 25 yds. (2.4 x 22.9m), King 120" x 20 yds. (3 x 18.3m)

History of Wool

Merino, Rambouillet, Bluefaced Leicester, and Corriedale are the most common sheep for wool breeds. Once a year, the sheep are sheared of their wool coats, also called a fleece. The wool fleece is full of oil, lanolin, and debris. This is cleaned using soap, detergent, or an acid bath. The wool is teased or picked to open the locks. The wool fluff is blown into a room and bonded together using heat. Merino wool is better for spinning than making comforters.

Hobbs Bonded Fibers

• Heirloom Premium Wool
  PKG. SIZES: Queen 90" x 108" (2.3 x 2.7m), King 120" x 120" (3 x 3m)
  ROLL: 108" x 25 yds. (2.7 x 22.9m)

• Tuscany 100% Wool Batting (washable, resin bonded)
  PKG. SIZES: Crib 45" x 60" (1.2 x 1.5m), Throw 60" x 60" (1.5 x 1.5m), Twin 72" x 96" (1.8 x 2.4m), Full 81" x 96" (2.1 x 2.4m), Queen 96"x 108" (2.4 x 2.7m), King 120" x 120" (3 x 3m)
  ROLL: 96" x 30 yds. (2.4 x 27.4m)
  BOARD: 96" x 15 yds. (2.4 x 13.7m)

Pellon

• W – Wool High Loft Blend Batting (50% wool/50% polyester)
  PKG. SIZES: Craft: 34" x 45" (0.9 x 1.1m), Crib 45" x 60" (1.1 x 1.5m), Throw 60" x 60" (1.5 x 1.5m), Twin 72" x 96" (1.8 x 2.4m), Full 81" x 96" (2.1 x 2.4m), Queen 96" x 108" (2.4 x 2.7m), King 120" x 120" (3 x 3m)

ROLL: 90" x 6 yds. (2.3 x 5.5m), 90" x 30 yds. (2.3 x 27.4m), 96" x 30 yds. (2.4 x 27.4m), 120" x 30 yds. (3 x 27.4m)
BOLT: 90" x 6 yds. (2.3 x 5.5m), 90" x 9 yds. (2.3 x 8.2m), 96" x 9 yds. (2.4 x 8.2m)

- Z – 100% Wool Batting (needle punched with scrim)
  PKG. SIZES: Craft 34" x 45" (0.9 x 1.1m), Queen 90" x 108" (1.3 x 2.7m)
  ROLL: 90" x 6 yds. (2.3 x 5.5m), 90" x 30 yds. (2.3 x 27.4m)
  BOLT: 90" x 9 yds. (2.3 x 8.2m)

Fairfield
- Nature-Fil Wool Batting (100% sheep's wool)
  ROLL: 90" x 20 yds. (1.3 x 18.3m), 90" x 8 yds. (1.3 x 7.3m)

- Natural Wool (100% sheep's wool)
  PKG. SIZES: Twin 72" x 90" (1.8 x 1.3m), Queen 90" x 108" (1.3 x 2.7m)

Bosal
- Bigelow™ 100% Wool Batting (dry clean only)
  PKG. SIZES: Crib 45" x 60" (1.1 x 1.5m), Twin 72" x 94" (1.8 x 2.4m), Full 90" x 94" (1.3 x 2.4m), Queen 108" x 94" (2.7 x 2.4m)

Polyester

Polyester Batting

This is a synthetic fiber, it holds its shape, and makes some of the highest loft batting available, up to ½"–⅝" (1.3–1.6cm) thick. It comes in a wide range of weights and lofts, from flat and dense (almost like felt) to light, airy, and very thick or lofty.

It does not compress; is thicker but lighter. It has warmth without weight, resists mold and mildew, and does not shrink when washed. It is good for bed quilts, comforters, and any project where shrinkage would cause problems.

Is strong, stable, and resists mold and mildew. It is lightweight with superb insulation quality.

Comes in bright white (perfect for quilts with a lighter or white background fabric). It is also available in pure black (for quilts with a dark or black background fabric).

It is made from synthetic materials, and is a very high-quality fine denier polyester fiber. This makes it soft and stretchy; it'll take a tug but it retains its shape and has wonderful drape.

High loft polyester batting gives quilts an incredibly thick, fluffy look without adding a lot of weight. It can be quilted up to 4"–6" (10.2–15.3cm) apart. This is perfect for baby quilts, floor play mats, or any project where loft is desired.

Low loft polyester batting is very stable and flat, often as thin as 1/16" (0.2cm). It can be quilted up to 10"–12" (25.4–30.5cm) apart. It will not shrink when washed; this makes it perfect for table runners, place mats, bags, or other projects where a flat-structured look is desired.

It does not shrink when washed and it has no memory retention of folds and creases, this makes it a good choice for quilts that will be folded for shipping or stored for a season or two.

It is less expensive than natural fiber battings.

> It is good for hand or machine quilting, although the higher the loft the more difficult hand quilting would be.

> It is either bonded or needle punched to prevent bearding and fiber migration.

Disadvantages
- It is not a natural fiber.
- High heat can melt polyester batting; machine wash and dry finished quilts on cool temperature settings.
- May beard depending on the brand.

POLYESTER BATTING MANUFACTURERS

Quilters Dream Batting

• **Dream Poly® Request Thinnest Loft Batting**
PKG. SIZES: Craft 46" x 36" (1.2 x 0.9m), Crib 46" x 60" (1.2 x 1.5m), Throw 60" x 60" (1.5 x 1.5m), Twin 93" x 72" (2.3 x 1.8m), Double 96" x 93" (2.4 x 2.3m), Queen 108" x 93" (2.7 x 2.3m), Super Queen 93" x 121" (2.3 x 3.1m), King 122" x 120" (3.1 x 3m)
ROLL: Throw Roll 60" x 30 yds. (1.5 x 27.4m), Queen Roll 93" x 30 yds. (2.3 x 27.4m), King Roll 120" x 30 yds. (3 x 27.4m)
BOLT: Runner Bolt 18" x 30 yds. (0.5 x 27.4m), Baby Bolt 46" x 15 yds. (1.2 x 13.7m), Throw Bolt 60" x 15 yds. (1.5 x 13.7m)

• **Dream Poly Select Mid Loft Batting**
PKG. SIZES: Craft 46" x 36" (1.2 x 0.9m), Crib 46" x 60" (1.2 x 1.5m), Throw 60" x 60" (1.5 x 1.5m), Twin 93" x 72" (2.3 x 1.8m), Double 96" x 93" (2.4 x 2.3), Queen 108" x 93" (2.7 x 2.3m), Super Queen 93" x 121" (2.3 x 3.1m), King 122" x 120" (3.1 x 3m)

ROLL: Throw Roll 60" x 30 yds. (1.5 x 27.4m), Queen Roll 93" x 30 yds. (2.3 x 27.4m), King Roll 120" x 25 yds. (3 x 22.9m)

BOLT: Runner Bolt 18" x 30 yds. (0.5 x 27.4m), Baby Bolt 46" x 15 yds. (1.2 x 13.7m), Throw Bolt 61" x 15 yds. (1.5 x 13.7m)

• **Dream Poly Deluxe Weighty Loft Batting**
PKG. SIZES: Craft 46" x 36" (1.2 x 0.9m), Crib 46" x 60" (1.2 x 1.5m), Throw 60" x 60" (1.5 x 1.5m), Twin 93" x 72" (2.3 x 1.8m), Double 96" x 93" (2.4 x 2.3m), Queen 108" x 93" (2.7 x 2.3m), Super Queen 93" x 121" (2.3 x 3.1m), King 122" x 120" (3.1 x 3m)
ROLL: Throw Roll 60" x 30 yds. (1.5 x 27.4m), Queen Roll 93" x 30 yds. (2.3 x 27.4m), King Roll 120" x 25 yds. (3 x 22.9m)

• **Dream Poly Select Mid Loft Batting (black)**
PKG. SIZES: Craft 46" x 36" (1.2 x 0.9m), Crib 46" x 60" (1.2 x 1.5m), Throw 60" x 60" (1.5 x 1.5m), Twin 93" x 72" (2.3 x 1.8m), Double 96" x 93" (2.4 x 2.3m), Queen 108" x 93" (2.7 x 2.3m), Super Queen 93" x 121" (2.3 x 3.1m), King 122" x 120" (3.1 x 3m)
ROLL: Queen Roll 93" x 30 yds. (2.3 x 27.4m), King Roll 120" x 25 yds. (3 x 22.9m)

• **Dream Angel™ Select Mid Loft Batting (flame-retardant fibers)**
PKG. SIZES: Craft 46" x 36" (1.2 x 0.9m), Crib 46" x 60" (1.2 x 1.5m), Throw 60" x 60" (1.5 x 1.5m), Twin 93" x 72" (2.3 x 1.8m), Double 96" x 93" (2.4 x 2.3m), Queen 108" x 93" (2.7 x 2.3m), Super Queen 93" x 121" (2.3 x 3.1m), King 122" x 120" (3.1 x 3m)
ROLL: Queen Roll 93" x 30 yds. (2.3 x 27.4m), King Roll 120" x 30 yds. (3 x 27.4m)

BOLT: Baby Bolt 46" x 15 yds. (1.2 x 13.7m), Throw Bolt 60" x 15 yds. (1.5 x 13.7m)

- **Dream Green™ Select Mid Loft Batting**
  PKG. SIZES: Craft 46" x 36" (1.2 x 0.9m), Crib 46" x 60" (1.2 x 1.5m), Throw 60" x 60" (1.5 x 1.5m), Twin 93" x 72" (2.3 x 1.8m), Double 96" x 93" (2.4 x 2.3m), Queen 108" x 93" (2.7 x 2.3m), Super Queen 93" x 121" (2.3 x 3.1m), King 122" x 120" (3.1 x 3m)
  ROLL: Queen Roll 93" x 30 yds. (2.3 x 27.4m), King Roll 120" x 25 yds. (3 x 22.9m)
  BOLT: Baby Bolt 46" x 15 yds. (1.2 x 13.7m), Throw Bolt 61" x 15 yds. (1.5 x 13.7m)

- **Dream Puff Batting**
  PKG. SIZES: Craft 46" x 36" (1.2 x 0.9m), Crib 46" x 60" (1.2 x 1.5m), Throw 60" x 60" (1.5 x 1.5m), Twin 93" x 72" (2.3 x 1.8m), Double 96" x 93" (2.4 x 2.3m), Queen 108" x 93" (2.7 x 2.3m), Super Queen 93" x 121" (2.3 x 3.1m), King 122" x 120" (3.1 x 3m)
  ROLL: Queen Roll 93" x 25 yds. (2.3 x 22.9m), King Roll 120" x 20 yds. (3 x 22.9m)

Hobbs Bonded Fibers
- **Cloudloft® Batting (resin-bonded, siliconized)**
  PKG. SIZES: Crib 45" x 60" (1.1 x 1.5m), Full 81" x 96" (2.1 x 2.4m), Queen 90" x 108" (2.3 x 2.7m), King 120" x 120" (3 x 3m)

- **Poly-Down Polyester Batting (100% polyester)**
  PKG. SIZES: Crib 45" x 60" (1.1 x 1.5m), Twin 72" x 96" (1.8 x 2.4m), Full 81" x 96" (2.1 x 2.4m), Queen 96" x 108" (2.4 x 2.7m), King 120" x 120" (3 x 3m)
  ROLL: 108" x 30 yds. (2.7 x 27.4m), 120" x 30 yds. (3 x 27.4m)

- Thermore® Batting (bonded)
  PKG. SIZES: Queen 90" x 108" (2.3 x 2.7m)
  ROLL: 45" x 25 yds. (1.1 x 22.9m)

- Tuscany 100% Premium Polyester Batting (resin bonded, siliconized)
  PKG. SIZES: Crib 45" x 60" (1.1 x 1.5m), Throw 60" x 60" (1.5 x 1.5m), Twin 72" x 96" (1.8 x 2.4m), Full 81" x 96" (2.1 x 2.4m), Queen 96" x 108" (2.4 x 2.7m), King 120" x 120" (3 x 3m)
  BOARD: 96" x 10 yds. (2.4 x 9.1m), 96" x 30 yds. (2.4 x 27.4m)

Pellon
- TP970 Thermolam® Plus Sew-In (NPP needle-punched polyester)
  PKG. SIZES: Crib 45" x 60" (1.1 x 1.5m)
  ROLL: 45" x 75 yds. (1.1 x 68.6m), 90" x 30 yds. (2.3 x 27.4m), 90" x 6 yds. (2.3 x 5.5)
  BOLT: 45" x 20 yds. (1.1 x 22.9m)

- 972 Econo-Fleece™ (100% polyester)
  BOLT: 45" x 20 yds. (1.1 x 22.9m)

- 988 Sew-In Fleece (100% polyester, low loft)
  PKG. SIZES: 22" x 36" (0.6 x 0.9m)
  ROLL: 45" x 80 yds. (1.1 x 73.2m)
  BOLT: 45" x 20 yds. (1.1 x 22.9m)

- P – Quilter's Touch 100% Polyester Batting – High Loft
  PKG. SIZES: Craft 34" x 45" (0.9 x 1.1m), Crib 45" x 60" (1.1 x 1.5m), Throw 60" x 60" (1.5 x 1.5m), Twin 72" x 96" (1.8 x 2.4m), Full 81" x 96" (2.1 x 2.4m), Queen 90" x 108" (2.3 x 2.7m), Super Queen 96" x 108" (2.4 x 2.7m), King 120" x 120" (3 x 3m)

ROLL: 90" x 6 yds. (2.3 x 5.4m), 90" x 30 yds.
(2.3 x 27.4m), 96" x 30 yds. (2.4 x 27.4m), 120" x 30 yds.
(3 x 27.4m)
BOLT: 90" x 6 yds. (2.3 x 5.4m), 90" x 9 yds. (2.3 x 8.2m),
96" x 9 yds. (2.4 x 8.2m)

- Y6 – 100% Polyester Batting – High Loft: Low
  ROLL: 96" x 30 yds. (2.4 x 27.4m)

- Y9 – 100% Polyester Batting – High Loft: Medium
  ROLL: 96" x 25 yds. (2.4 x 22.9m)

- Y12 – 100% Polyester Batting – High Loft: Heavy
  ROLL: 96" x 20 yds. (2.4 x 18.3m)

Fairfield
- Poly-Fil Rolled Stock 100% Polyester Batting (bonded)
  ROLL: 96" x 15 yds. (2.4 x 13.7m)

- Poly-Fil Feather Weight Batting Roll
  ROLL: 48" x 60 yds. (1.2 x 54.9m), 96" x 30 yds.
  (2.4 x 27.4m)

- Poly-Fil Light-Weight Batting
  ROLL: 48" x 45 yds. (1.2 x 41.1m)

- Poly-Fil Mid-Weight Batting
  ROLL: 48" x 30 yds. (1.2 x 27.4m), 96" x 15 yds.
  (2.4 x 13.7m)

- Poly-Fil Feather Loft Batting
  ROLL: 90" x 30 yds. (2.3 x 27.4m)

- **Poly-Fil Heavy-Weight Batting**
  ROLL: 48" x 22 yds. (1.2 x 20.1m), 96" x 11 yds. (2.4 x 10.1m)

- **Poly-Fil Ultra-Weight Batting**
  ROLL: 48" x 18 yds. (1.2 x 16.5m), 96" x 9 yds. (2.4 x 8.2m)

- **Poly-Fil Whisper-loft**
  PKG. SIZE: Crib 45" x 60" (1.1 x 1.5m), Twin 72" x 90" (1.8 x 2.3m), Full 81" x 96" (2.1 x 2.4m), Queen 90" x 108" (2.3 x 2.7m), King 120" x 120" (3 x 3m)

- **Poly-Fil Low-Loft® Batting (100% bonded polyester)**
  PKG. SIZE: Crib 45" x 60" (1.1 x 1.5m), Twin 72" x 90" (1.8 x 2.3m), Full 81" x 96" (2.1 x 2.4m), Queen 90" x 108" (2.3 x 2.7m), King 120" x 120" (3 x 3m)
  ROLL: 90" x 6 yds. (2.3 x 5.5m)

- **Poly-Fil Extra-Loft® Batting (100% bonded polyester)**
  PKG. SIZE: Craft 36" x 45" (0.9 x 1.1m), Crib 45" x 60" (1.1 x 1.5m), Twin 72" x 90" (1.8 x 2.3m), Full 81" x 96" (2.1 x 2.4m), Queen 90" x 108" (2.3 x 2.7m), King 120" x 120" (3 x 3m)
  ROLL: 45" x 50 yds. (1.1 x 1.3m), 90" x 6 yds. (2.3 x 5.5m)

- **Poly-Fil Hi-Loft® Batting (100% bonded polyester)**
  PKG. SIZE: Crib 45" x 60" (1.1 x 1.5m), Twin 72" x 90" (1.8 x 2.3m), Full 81" x 96" (2.1 x 2.4m), Queen 90" x 108" (2.3 x 2.7m), King 120" x 120" (3 x 3m)
  ROLL: 45" x 20 yds. (1.1 x 18.3m)

- **Poly-Fil Project Fleece™ Batting (100% polyester, needle punched)**
  PKG. SIZE: Craft 36" x 45" (0.9 x 1.1m), Crib 45" x 60" (1.1 x 1.5m), Twin 72" x 90" (1.8 x 2.3m), Full 81" x 96"

(2.1 x 2.4m), Queen 90" x 108" (2.3 x 2.7m), King
120" x 120" (3 x 3m)
ROLL: 90" x 6 yds. (2.3 x 5.5m), 120" x 120" (3 x 3m),
90" x 40 yds. (2.3 x 36.6m)

- **Poly-Fil Traditional® Fleece Batting**
  ROLL: 45" x 75 yds. (1.1 x 68.6m), 90" x 30 yds. (2.3 x 27.4m)

- **American Spirit Batting Premium Polyester (100% polyester,
  resin bonded)**
  PKG. SIZE: Crib 45" x 60" (1.1 x 1.5m)

Bosal
- **Katahdin Premium Quilt Batting (100% polyester, Winter 4.5 oz.)**
  PKG. SIZES: Queen 108" x 90" (2.7 x 2.3m)
  ROLL: 90" x 30 yds. (2.3 x 27.4m), 90" x 96 yds. (2.3 x 87.8m)

- **Powder Fill Ultra-Thin Polyester Batting**
  ROLL: 62" x 10 yds. (1.6 x 9.1m)

The Warm Company
- **Soft & Bright® Polyester Batting (100% polyester, needle punched)**
  PKG. SIZES: Crib 45" x 60" (1.1 x 1.5m), Twin 72" x 90"
  (1.8 x 2.3m), Full 90" x 96" (2.3 x 2.4m), Queen
  90" x 108" (2.3 x 2.7m), King 120" x 124" (3 x 3.1m)
  BOLT: 124" x 20 yds. (3.1 x 18.3m)

Fusible Batting

Fusible batting has been treated on one or both sides with a fusible layer that will adhere to fabric when heated with an iron. This essentially acts as the basting mechanism, instead of pin- or spray-basting, saving time and getting you to the quilting stage faster.

Single-sided fusible batting can be pressed into place with just one layer of fabric (the quilt top or the quilt back). Layer the batting fusible side up then smooth the fabric layer over it. Press the layers together one section at a time for 5–7 seconds before moving the iron to the next section.

Double-sided fusible batting can be layered between the quilt top and back and then pressed (not ironed) into place. Pressing gets the heat all the way through the layers by letting the iron sit in one spot for 5–7 seconds before moving it to the next spot.

If needed, some are manufactured with a water-soluble fusible material that washes away in the first laundering.

Comes in two main fibers, polyester and cotton blend. Polyester will not shrink after washing, but cotton blend will shrink up to 3–5% after washing.

Polyester fusible batting can be quilted up to 10" (25.4cm) apart, although about 4" (10.2cm) is recommended, cotton-blend fusible should be quilted up to 4" (10.2cm) apart.

Disadvantages
- Not ideal for hand quilting; the fusible layer may impede the needle.
- Harder to use for large projects. It will work for bed quilts, but it might be more difficult to iron bigger projects as they are more cumbersome, and it needs to be heated evenly all the way through.
- Made with glue or resin that is not a natural material.

Is perfect for smaller projects, such as table runners, place mats, bags, garments, tree skirts, and wall hangings.

FUSIBLE BATTING MANUFACTURERS

Quilters Dream Batting

• Fusible 80/20 (80% cotton/20% fine polyester with fusible webbing)

PKG. SIZES: Craft 46" x 36" (1.2 x 0.9m), Crib 60" x 46" (1.5 x 1.2m), Throw 46" x 60" (1.2 x 1.5m), Twin 93" x 72" (2.4 x 1.8m)

ROLL: 24" x 30 yds. (0.6 x 27.4m), 93" x 30 yds. (2.3 x 27.4m), 120" x 30 yds. (3 x 27.4m)

BOLT: Baby Bolt 46" x 15 yds. (1.2 x 13.7m), Throw Bolt 60" x 15 yds. (1.5 x 13.7m)

Hobbs Bonded Fibers

• Heirloom Premium 80/20 Fusible Cotton/Poly Batting (80% cotton/ 20% polyester)

PKG. SIZES: Crib 45" x 60" (1.2 x 1.5m), Queen 90" x 108" (2.3 x 2.7m)

ROLL: 96" x 30 yds. (2.4 x 27.4m)

Pellon

• 986F – Lightweight Fusible Fleece (100% polyester, low loft, one sided)

BOLT: 45" x 20 yds. (1.2 x 18.3m)

• 987F – Fusible Fleece (100% polyester, low loft, one sided)

PKG. SIZES: Crib 45" x 60" (1.2 x 1.5m)

BOLT: 45" x 20 yds. (1.2 x 18.3m), 45" x 15 yds. (1.2 x 13.7m)

MINI BOLT: 22" x 7 yds. (0.6 x 6.4m)

• 985F – Sandwich Fuse (100% polyester, low loft fleece, two sided, fusible)

PKG. SIZES: Crib 45" x 60" (1.2 x 1.5m)

BOLT: 45" x 20 yds. (1.2 x 18.3m)

- **973F – Heavyweight Fusible Fleece** (100% polyester, high loft fleece, one sided, fusible)
  BOLT: 45" x 10 yds. (1.2 x 9.1m)

- **TP971 – Fusible Thermolam® Plus** (100% polyester, heavily needled fleece)
  PKG. SIZES: Crib 45" x 60" (1.2 x 1.5m)
  BOLT: 45" x 15 yds. (1.2 x 13.7m)

- **X – 100% Fusible Polyester Batting – High Loft**
  PKG. SIZES: Craft 34" x 45" (0.9 x 1.1m), Crib 45" x 60" (1.1 x 1.5m), Throw 60" x 60" (1.5 x 1.5m), Twin 72" x 90" (1.8 x 2.3m), Full 81" x 96" (2.1 x 2.4m), Queen 90" x 108" (2.3 x 2.7m), King 120" x 120" (3 x 3m)
  ROLL: 60" x 6 yds. (1.5 x 5.5m), 90" x 6 yds. (2.3 x 5.5m), 60" x 30 yds. (1.5 x 27.4m), 90" x 30 yds. (2.3 x 27.4m)
  BOLT: 60" x 9 yds. (1.5 x 8.2m), 90" x 9 yds. (2.3 x 8.2m)

Fairfield
- **Fusi-Boo® Blended Fusible Batting** (rayon from bamboo and natural cotton)
  PKG. SIZES: Queen/King 100" x 116" (2.5 x 2.9m)

Bosal
- **Double-Sided Fusible Batting** (100% polyester)
  ROLL: 45" x 25 yds. (1.1 x 22.9m)

- **Duet Fuse II Double-Sided Fusible Batting** (100% polyester fleece)
  PKG. SIZES: Craft 36" x 45" (0.9 x 1.1m), Crib 45" x 60" (1.1 x 1.5m)
  ROLL: 45" x 25 yds. (1.1 x 22.9m), 2½" x 20 yds. (6.35cm x 18.3m)

- **Single-Sided Light Fusible Batting** (100% polyester)
  ROLL: 45" x 25 yds. (1.1 x 22.9m)

Resources

The following manufacturers make and/or sell the battings listed in this guide. You can find these brands and others online and at your local craft/sewing retailers.

- Quilters Dream® Batting
  (*www.QuiltersDreamBatting.com*)

- Hobbs Bonded Fibers (*www.HobbsBatting.com*)

- Pellon® (*www.PellonProjects.com*)

- Fairfield™ (*www.FairfieldWorld.com*)

- Bosal™ (*www.BosalOnline.com*)

- The Warm Company® (*www.WarmCompany.com*)

Photo Credits

Front cover image by Mike Mihalo Photography.

Images from *www.Shutterstock.com*: arigato (all textured backgrounds in the footers, textured backgrounds in banners on pages 2, 13, 23, 31, 35, 39, 45, 57, 63, 64); Morphart Creation (3); Mike_O (background photo 13); Variya (background photo 23); AppleZoomZoom (background photo 31); ICHWAN SATRIA ATMAJA (background photo 35); MoonBloom (background photo 39); tanaphongpict (background photo 45); fotosv (background photo 57).

About the Author

KRISTA MOSER is the creative force and inspiration behind Krista Moser, The Quilted Life (*www.KristaMoser.com*). She has published more than two dozen patterns since 2016 and created the 60 Degree Diamond Rulers for Creative Grids.

A quilting and fiber arts enthusiast, Krista started sewing at eight years old. She began her professional sewing and machine-quilting career at the spunky age of fourteen, adding the texture and dimension machine quilting brings to every project.